# Alto Saxophone Student

## by Fred Weber in collaboration with Willis Coggins

## To The Student

Level II of the Belwin "Student Instrumental Course" is a continuation of Level I of this series or may be used to follow any other good elementary instruction book. It is designed to help you become an excellent player on your instrument in a most enjoyable manner. It will take a reasonable amount of work and CAREFUL practice on your part. If you do this, learning to play should be a valuable and pleasant experience.

Please see top of Page 3 for practice suggestions and other comments that should be very helpful.

## To The Teacher

Level II of this series is a continuation of the Belwin "Student Instrumental Course", which is the first and only complete course for individual instruction of all band instruments. Like instruments may be taught in classes. Cornets, Trombones, Baritones and Basses may be taught together. The course is designed to give the student a sound musical background and, at the same time, provide for the highest degree of interest and motivation. The entire course is correlated to the band oriented sequence.

Each page of this book is planned as a complete lesson, however, because some students advance more rapidly than others, and because other lesson situations may vary, lesson assignments are left to the discretion of the teacher.

To make the course both authoritative and practical, most books are co-authored by a national authority of each instrument in collaboration with Fred Weber, perhaps the most widely-known and accepted authority at the student level.

The Belwin "Student Instrumental Course" has three levels: elementary, intermediate, and advanced intermediate. Each level consists of a method and three correlating supplementary books. In addition, a duet book is available for Flute, B♭ Clarinet, E♭ Alto Sax, B♭ Cornet and Trombone. The chart below shows the correlating books available with each part.

---

The Belwin "STUDENT INSTRUMENTAL COURSE" - A course for individual and class instruction of LIKE instruments, at three levels, for all band instruments.

*EACH BOOK IS COMPLETE IN ITSELF BUT ALL BOOKS ARE CORRELATED WITH EACH OTHER*

**METHOD**
**"The Alto Saxophone Student"**
For individual or class instruction

*ALTHOUGH EACH BOOK CAN BE USED SEPARATELY, IDEALLY, ALL SUPPLEMENTARY BOOKS SHOULD BE USED AS COMPANION BOOKS WITH THE METHOD*

| STUDIES & MELODIOUS ETUDES | TUNES FOR TECHNIC | ALTO SAXOPHONE SOLOS | DUETS FOR STUDENTS |
|---|---|---|---|
| Supplementary scales, warm-up and technical drills, musicianship studies and melody-like etudes, all carefully correlated with the method. | Technical type melodies, variations, and "famous passages" from musical literature for the development of — technical dexterity. | Four separate correlated Solos, with piano accompaniment, written or arranged by Willis Coggins:<br><br>To a Wild Rose . . *MacDowell*<br>Aria . . . . . . . . . . . *Coggins*<br>Berceuse. . . . . . . . .*Ilyinsky*<br>Gavotte . . . . . . . . . *Gluck* | A book of carefully correlated duet arrangements of interesting and familiar melodies without piano accompaniments.<br>Available for:   Flute<br>                B♭ Clarinet<br>                Alto Sax<br>                B♭ Cornet<br>                Trombone |

# CORRELATED SAXOPHONE SOLOS

Four separate solos, with piano accompaniment, were selected and arranged specifically for this course. We strongly encourage the use of these solos as supplementary lesson material.

**TO A WILD ROSE** .... Edward MacDowell
*arr. by Willis Coggins*

**ARIA** ................................ Willis Coggins

**BERCEUSE** ................ Alexander Ilyinsky
*arr. by Willis Coggins*

**GAVOTTE** .................. Chr. W. von Gluck
*arr. by Willis Coggins*

---

# SAXOPHONE FINGERING CHART

When a number is given, refer to the picture of the Saxophone for additional keys to be pressed.

When two ways to finger a note are given, the first way is the one most often used. The second fingering is for use in special situations.

When two notes are given together (F♯ and G♭) they are the same tone and, of course, played the same way.

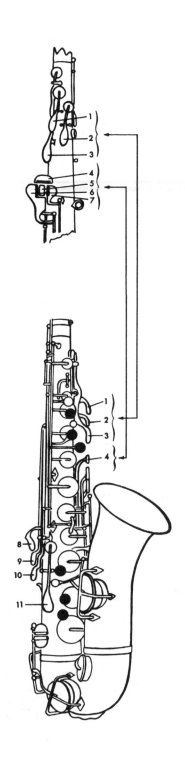

## A Few Important Practice Suggestions

1. Set a regular practice time and make every effort to practice at this time.

2. ALWAYS practice carefully. Careless practice is a waste of time. Learn to play each line exactly as written. Later there may be times when certain freedoms may be taken.

3. ALWAYS use a GOOD reed. When it is nicked or damaged in any way it should be discarded. The way to be economical with reeds is to take care of good reeds. Don't see how long you can still use them after they have been damaged.

4. The instrument must always be clean, in good playing condition, and all keys adjusted properly.

5. The development of careful and accurate playing habits is essential if you are to become a good player. Proper hand, finger, mouth or embouchure, and body position is absolutely necessary for best results. Always keep relaxed.

6. COUNT AT ALL TIMES.

*Remember — Music should be fun but the better player you are the more*
*fun you have. It takes work to become a good player.*

## Daily Warm-Up Studies

The lines below are intended for use as daily warm-up drill, rhythm and dynamic studies, and for the development of technical proficiency. They should be used as an addition or supplement to the regular lesson assignment.

Use certain lines as a daily routine with changes from time to time as suggested by your teacher.

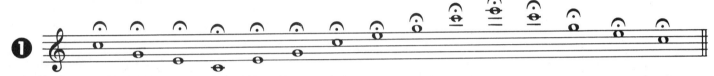

Use the above tones in the following manner:

1. As long tones — Hold each note as long as comfortable. Listen carefully for your best tone and keep the tone steady.

2. Play each tone using various shadings as indicated in Ⓐ , Ⓑ , and Ⓒ below. (number ❷)

3. Use Pattern Ⓓ (number ❷ below) on each scale tone — first staccato, then with accents.

TONGUING — Play line 3 on all the tones in line 1.

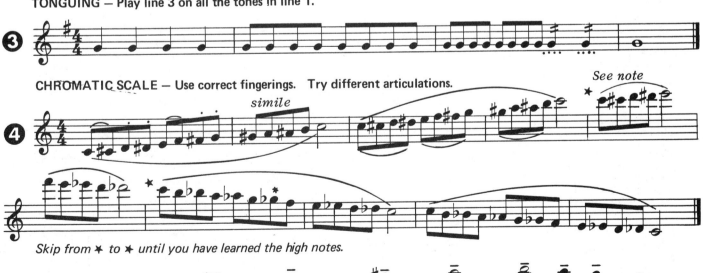

*Play slowly and listen carefully.*

B.I.C.231

4

6/10/03

Warm-up.   Play slowly and listen carefully.   Keep tone steady.

*Always play with your most pleasant sounding tone.   Take lots of time while practicing Number 1 and listen carefully as you play.   Correct practicing of Number 1 should take much more time than any other study on the page.*

**G Major Scale**

**Thirds in G Major**

*Work out slowly, then try for speed.*

**STACCATO**          **LEGATO**          **ACCENTS**

**Slowly — observe markings carefully.**

## Emperor Waltz Theme

**Slow waltz tempo**

STRAUSS

*Breathe only at commas; they mark the phrases.*

B.I.C.231

Remember — Some notes on the saxophone can be fingered more than one way. These additional fingerings are usually called "alternate fingerings". In the line below we use what is commonly called the chromatic fingering for F♯ (or G♭). It is usually used when F♯ or G♭ is approached by half steps either from above or below. It is very important to know <u>how</u> and <u>when</u> to use alternate fingerings. They lead to faster and smoother playing as you progress. Even though the regular fingerings may seem easier at this point, you must learn to use the alternate fingerings in the proper places. They are absolutely essential in faster and more advanced playing.

\* — Means to use the alternate fingering. It will be used for a few pages to remind you — it is never used in regular band music.

*means — use alternate fingering.*

**CHROMATIC SCALE**

*It is a common practice to write sharps when going up the chromatic scale and flats coming down.*

## Long Long Ago

**INTERVAL VARIATION** — The accented notes below sound a familiar melody. Make certain these tones stand out.

## Vilia

Many saxophone players can play a lot of notes rapidly. However, the true test of a good player is whether or not he can play a song-like melody with beauty, style, proper expression and phrasing. On all song-like melodies work primarily to achieve beauty, expression, and a singing quality. Don't just play notes.

LEHAR

B.I.C.231

Check "TUNES FOR SAXOPHONE TECHNIC" for more melodies that provide technical development.

**C Major Scale**

**1**

**Thirds in C Major**

**2**

*Play bottom octave first time — top octave on repeat.*        *Play top octave first time — bottom octave on repeat.*

**3**

**4**

**SCALE COUNTING FUN**

**5**

Sometimes abbreviations are used in writing music.   In the line below a BAR across the stem means to divide the note into eighth notes (two BARS would mean Sixteenth notes).   Frequently, but not always, dots are used to indicate how many tones the note is divided into.

**6**

## Hornpipe

TRADITIONAL

**Work for smooth octave changes.**

**7**

## To A Wild Rose

**A PHRASING STUDY**

MAC DOWELL

**Strive for beauty — Tongue softly when necessary, but keep the tongue flowing.**

**8**

*Fine*

*D. C. al Fine*

If you have not already done so, please see the book "STUDIES AND MELODIOUS ETUDES" for more scale and technical studies that correlate with Method Book II.

**REVIEW NOTE ON ALTERNATE FINGERING AT TOP OF PAGE 5.**
*See page 48 for a summary of all common alternate fingerings.*

Alternate F#        Regular F#

* means — use alternate fingering.    Memorize when alternate fingering should be used.

Play 3 times — then last note.        Play 3 times — then last note.

Review in case you have forgotten.  Add Octave Key for Top Octave.        same        same

same fingering        same        same        same        same

open

bottom octave    top octave

## Devils Dream

MELODY FOR PRACTICING REGISTER CHANGE        TRADITIONAL

8

Apply pattern to each tone.

①

Play the above pattern on all tones of the C scale by memory.

ARPEGGIOS

②

③

1 e + a 2 +

Tonguing fun with Skaters Waltz.   Strive for fast but light tonguing.

④

## Little Brown Jug - Theme and Variation

TRADITIONAL

MELODY

⑤

SCALE VARIATION IN KEY OF G — Work out slowly; then try for speed.

The line below is a REVIEW of the matter of separating or spacing notes. Not separating notes, when they should be separated, is one of the most common errors made by young players. Separating or spacing notes means there must be a slight rest or silence between each note. This is done by a short stoppage of air between the notes. Staccato and accent marks usually indicate the notes are to be separated. The style of the piece also determines this. When learning to play with separation, it will help first to play the notes slowly with a rest between each note. Then speed up using the same style of playing.

As written:

As played:

**❶**

Tone Diagrams

*Play in a light staccato manner.*

**❷**

**❸**

**❹**

Write counting under notes, then play.

**❺**

Count:   1 + 2 +

## Dance From The Nutcracker Suite

TSCHAIKOWSKY

**❻**

*rit.*

\* — *Use alternate fingering for C.*
\*\* — *See note Page 21, No. 4*

B.I.C.231

**Scale of F Major**

## Dotted Eighth And Sixteenth Notes

There are numerous ways to learn how to count dotted eighth and sixteenth notes ( ♪. ♫ ). USE THE SYSTEM PREFERRED BY YOUR TEACHER. This procedure is suggested by the author: Think DOWN - UP with the foot, on the dotted eighth note, the sixteenth note being played _after_ the UP beat, midway between the UP and the next DOWN. The UP beat MUST come in the exact center or middle of the count. Sometimes it helps to think of the sixteenth note as coming BEFORE the note it PRECEDES rather than AFTER the dotted eighth it follows.

### Country Gardens

TRADITIONAL

* If ties give trouble, play first without ties.

**Two alternate fingerings for B♭. (Add octave key for top octave)**

*Double Key*     *One and One*

*Double Key*     *Side B♭ (regular)*

**Thirds in F Major**   *Double Key*

**CHROMATIC SCALE**

**SYNCOPATION**

## Our Boys Will Shine Tonight

**Fun with counting.**

## Red River Valley

## Lil' Liza Jane

B.I.C.231

*Only notes marked * are played with the alternate fingering.*

The alternate fingering for C♯, (3rd space) is presented below so you will become familiar with it. There are times when it is helpful. It is frequently used on faster passages when going from D to C♯ and back to D. Otherwise it would be necessary to raise all fingers to play the open C♯. In many cases, some teachers prefer to alternate while others prefer the regular fingering for C♯. Use the fingering preferred by your teacher.

Theme From Gypsy Baron

STRAUSS

**Scale of D Major**

**Thirds in D Major**

*Play bottom octave first time — top octave on repeat.*    *Play top octave first time — bottom octave on repeat.*

## Barcarolle

Slow **6/8** tune.   6 counts per measure. ♪ = 1 count

OFFENBACH

* *see note below*

To nest strain | Fine ending

D. C. al Fine

\* *Give special attention to getting a nice tone on the high notes and in playing them in tune.*

ETUDE — Play using a light, staccato style

## Slow And Fast ⁶⁄₈ Time

When a piece in ⁶⁄₈ time goes quite fast, it is difficult to count out all 6 beats. We simplify this on ⁶⁄₈ tunes that are played fast by counting only 2 counts per measure. In this book, pieces in which we count out all 6 beats will be referred to as SLOW ⁶⁄₈ , and those we count in 2 beats per measure will be FAST ⁶⁄₈ . The counting written under the notes in the line below shows you the comparison between counting slow and fast ⁶⁄₈ time. You will note that in FAST ⁶⁄₈ time there are 3 eighth notes ( ♪♪♪ ) to a beat and a ♩. receives one beat.

Practice in both slow and fast ⁶⁄₈ time.

### Sailing Sailing

MARKS

### Our Director March

BIGELOW

Apply to scale.

**COUNTING RESTS**

*Stars And Stripes Forever Melody*

SOUSA

## Minor Scales And Scale Review

There is a minor scale corresponding with every major scale and having the same key signature. This is called the Relative Minor. By starting on the 6th tone of a major scale, using the same key signature and playing an octave, we have a minor scale. Although there are three forms of the minor scale, only two forms, harmonic and melodic are frequently used. The harmonic form follows the key signature except the 7th tone is raised one-half step both going up and coming down. In the melodic minor scale, when going up, the 6th and 7th tones are raised one-half step from what is indicated in the key signature. Coming down it follows the key signature.

Both the Harmonic and melodic forms of minor are used below in the four most common minor keys. Practice and study them carefully so you understand how they are formed. Try to become familiar with their sound.

B.I.C.231

**Minor Etudes**

a minor

Slowly — with expression

*Hungarian Dance No. 4 ***

BRAHMS

Dramatically — with feeling

Count: + 2 + 1

Lively, with spirit

* Is the above number in Major or minor?

On Wings Of Song

MENDELSSOHN

Pay special attention to playing all notes in tune, especially High A. This tune is in the Key of D. Actually it will sound better on your Sax — one note lower in the Key of C but you need practice on making it sound well in this key. Try transposing it one note lower to the Key of C — no sharps or flats.

B.I.C.231

**FINGERING DRILLS**

*Repeat each drill three times.*

*Counting must be steady and even.*

*like B♭*

## Russian Sailor Dance

**Moderately fast**

*Fine*

*D. C. al Fine*

## Grace Notes

A Grace note is a very short note played lightly just before the main or accented note. In most grace note situations, the grace note is played just before the beat; with the main note coming on the beat. There is a variation of this but we aren't concerned with it at this time.

grace note

## Gavotte

**Allegro moderato**                                                                 GOSSEC

*In a light staccato style.*

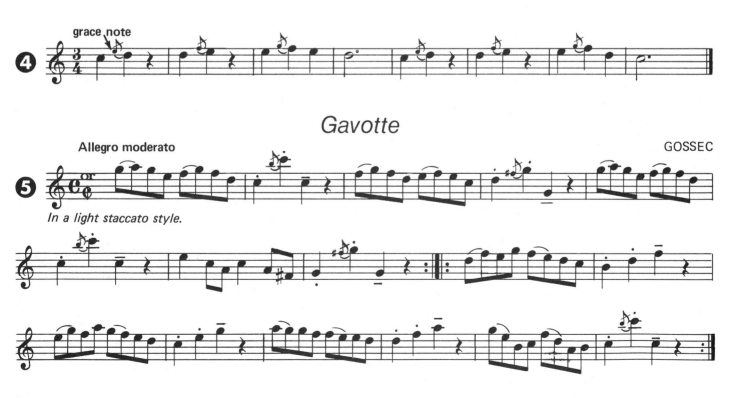

22

**OCTAVES**

*Listen carefully and be sure octaves are perfectly in tune.*

## Arpeggio Waltz

*Work up to a fairly rapid tempo.*

**Emphasize accented notes.**

## Sonatina

**Moderato — with expression**

BEETHOVEN

*mp*

*Fine*

*D.C. al Fine*

**Bb Major Scale**

**Thirds in Bb Major**

*Also tongue all notes staccato*

**ETUDE**

**A TONGUING TUNE**

## The Man On The Flying Trapeze

TRADITIONAL

*Use light tonguing and work for speed.*

## Humoresque

**Moderato — smoothly, like a song.**

DVORAK

*Review comments on Dotted Eighth and Sixteenth notes on Page 10.*

*Fine f*

*D.C. al Fine*

B.I.C.231

24

*Garry Owens*

TRADITIONAL

## Hurricane

**Very fast in strict tempo**

*Fine*

*D.C. al Fine*

## Beautiful Dreamer

*See note before VILIA on Page 5.*

S. FOSTER

**With expression**

*Play smoothly in a song-like manner.*

Scale of A Major

Thirds in A Major

Work for speed with accruacy

COUNTING ETUDE

## Cielito Lindo

A TONGUING TUNE  
Rather fast

FERNANDEZ

*Use a short, light tongue stroke.*

## Irish Washerwoman

2 beats per measure

TRADITIONAL

Count: 1 2

B.I.C.231

28

**2 beats per measure**

*Work out slowly, then increase speed.*

Fine

D.C. al Fine

## March From The Nutcracker Suite

March-like, with spirit

TSCHAIKOWSKY

like F♮

B.I.C.231

CHROMATIC SCALE

❶ Use chromatic fingering.

FAST TONGUING ETUDE

❷ Light staccato tonguing style.

❸ like F♮

National Emblem March

BAGLEY

Trio — with spirit

❹ Count: 2 1

30

## Waltz From Coppelia

DELIBES

*\* See note below.*

*\* This melody would be easier in the Key of G (1 sharp) but it provides needed practice in this key of 3 sharps (A). Try playing it ONE note lower in the Key of G.*

Majestically — with spirit

Count carefully.

## Yankee Doodle Boy

COHAN

A COUNTING TUNE

## Norwegian Dance

GRIEG

In Key of C

Play lightly, with expression.

Work out slowly, then increase speed.

In Key of D

Work out slowly, then increase speed.

B.I.C.231

## Scale Review

Bb Major

g minor — Harmonic Form — Relative to Bb Major

g minor — Melodic Form

g minor — Arpeggio

A Major

f# minor — Harmonic Form — Relative to A Major

f# minor — Melodic Form

f# minor — Arpeggio

*like F♮*

g minor Etude

## Gypsy Melody

**A STUDY IN PHRASING**

SARASATE

Slowly and dramatically, with expression

*Is this melody in Major or minor mood?*

**Etude in g minor**

**TONGUING ETUDE**

*Play lightly*

*like B♭*

*rit.*

# Gopak

**Rather fast and vigorous**

RUSSIAN FOLK DANCE

*Work out carefully, then increase speed.*

*Fine*

*D. C. al Fine*

34

**E Major Scale**

**①**

**Thirds in E Major**

**②**

**③**

**④**

A TONGUING AND COUNTING TUNE *Oh! Susanna*

S. FOSTER

**⑤**

*Use light tongue strokes and work for speed.*

*The Jolly Swiss Boy*

Moderato

TRADITIONAL

*Fine*

*like Bb*

*D.C. al Fine*

35

## Andante Cantabile*

MENDELSSOHN

## Variation

## Hungarian Dance No. 6

BRAHMS

*Andante cantabile means — slowly in a singing style.*

B.I.C.231

**CHROMATIC SCALE**

**①** *Work out slowly, then try for speed.*

**STUDY IN E MAJOR**

**②** *simile*

**③** *etc.*

## Spanish Dance

MOSZKOWSKI

**Lively**

**④** *Practice first without grace notes.*

*Fine*

*D.C. al Fine*

**FAST TONGUING ETUDE** — light staccato style

Work out slowly, then increase speed.

## Minuet

BOCCHERINI

Not too fast

Count:  3   +   1   +   2   +   3   +   1
        3   +   1   +   2   +   3   +   1

rit. - - - -   a tempo

**Eb Major Scale**

**①**

**Thirds in Eb Major**

**②**

**③**

**④**

**A TONGUING TUNE — What melody is this based on?**

**⑤**

*Use a light tongue stroke and work for speed.*

*Fine*

*D.C. al Fine*

## Serenade

SCHUBERT

**Slowly — in a songlike manner.** When necessary, tongue in a soft, legato manner.

**⑥**

Count:  1    2 3  +    1    2 3  +    1 2  +  3

*rit.*

## Excerpts From William Tell

ROSSINI

CHROMATIC SCALE

Work out carefully, then try for speed.

ETUDE

## Won't You Come Home Bill Bailey?

TECHNIC TUNE (Dixieland style)

CANNON

Work out slowly, then increase speed.

**FAST TONGUING**

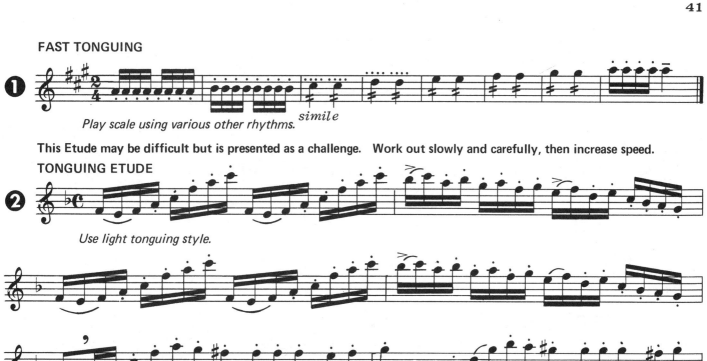

*Play scale using various other rhythms.* *simile*

This Etude may be difficult but is presented as a challenge. Work out slowly and carefully, then increase speed.

**TONGUING ETUDE**

*Use light tonguing style.*

## Melodies From Hungarian Rhapsody No. 2

LISZT

**Work out carefully, then play in a vigorous manner.**

*All repeats must be observed.*

**Counting Etude in b minor**

**①**

**ETUDE**

**②**

*Work out slowly, then increase speed.*

# Swan Lake

**Moderato**

TSCHAIKOWSKY

**③**

*With expression*

*rit.*

*a tempo*

# Arpeggios On Brahms Lullaby

This arpeggio etude is based upon the melody of "Brahms Lullaby". Work it out carefully and then increase speed. Emphasize the accented notes.

# Caprice

B.I.C.231

This page is intended to give the student an introductory knowledge and understanding of scales, scale structure and keys. The teacher is encouraged to expand on these ideas as he sees fit.

# Scales and Keys

We are frequently told to practice scales because it will make us better players. Practicing scales improves our finger dexterity; But there is another and probably more important reason.

A piece of music in a certain key is usually based on the scale containing the same sharps or flats. For instance, a tune in the key of F (1 flat in the key signature) is usually based on the scale of F which contains one flat. This relationship with the scale is the same for ALL keys. As we learn to play each scale, a certain fingering pattern is developed which greatly increases our ability to play in the key based on that scale. Our fingers grow accustomed to the fingering pattern of the key.

Since on a wind instrument there is no way of showing a complete picture of all the notes and their relationship to each other, the drawing of a piano or organ key board showing all the notes is printed below.

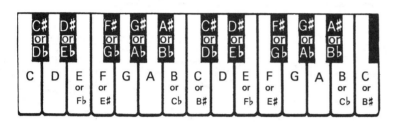

## Memorize

1. A half-step is the distance from any note to the closest note above or below, regardless of whether it is a black key or white key.
2. A whole-step is two half-steps.
3. ALL scales follow a definite pattern of half-steps and whole-steps.

The MAJOR scale is the most common scale and the only one we can be concerned with on this page. The major scale always follows this pattern of half-steps and whole-steps. *(notes of the scale)* **1  2  3  4  5  6  7  8**

*Steps between — —*  1  1  ½  1  1  1  ½

From this, you can see the half and whole-step pattern. 1  1  ½  1  1  1  ½ (2 whole steps and a half-step followed by 3 whole-steps and a half-step).

Each major scale has 8 tones and is one octave. It can be repeated over several octaves either down or up. From the keyboard diagram you can see that the scale starting on "C" follows this pattern without using any sharps or flats. This is why the scale of C and the key of C has no sharps or flats.

Scales can be started on any tone of the keyboard. By building alphabetically according to the major scale pattern of half and whole-steps (1  1  ½  1  1  1  ½), a major scale is formed.

EXAMPLE: Start on D-a whole-step above D is E — another whole-step is F♯ — a half-step up is G. A whole-step up is A— another whole-step is B and the next whole-step is C♯. We complete the scale with a half-step to D.

Our scale then is D E F♯ G A B C♯ D. This shows that the scale of D has two sharps and the key of D has this signature:

Build the following scales. Your teacher will help you. F, B♭, G, E♭, A.

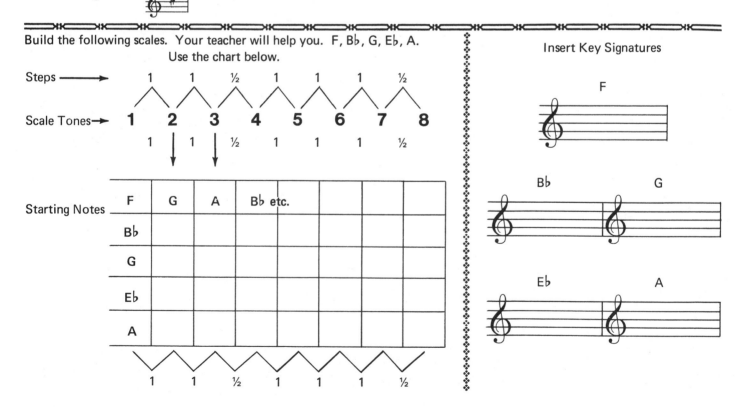

## Scales For Review Or Reference

ALL Minor scales are in the Harmonic Form.

## Scale Patterns

The scale patterns below provide unlimited scale and articulation practice in the seven most common band keys. Start with ANY number and play through the entire pattern, returning to the starting line and playing to where END is marked. End by holding the last note. KEEP THE STARTING KEY THROUGHOUT THE ENTIRE PATTERN. Use various articulations.

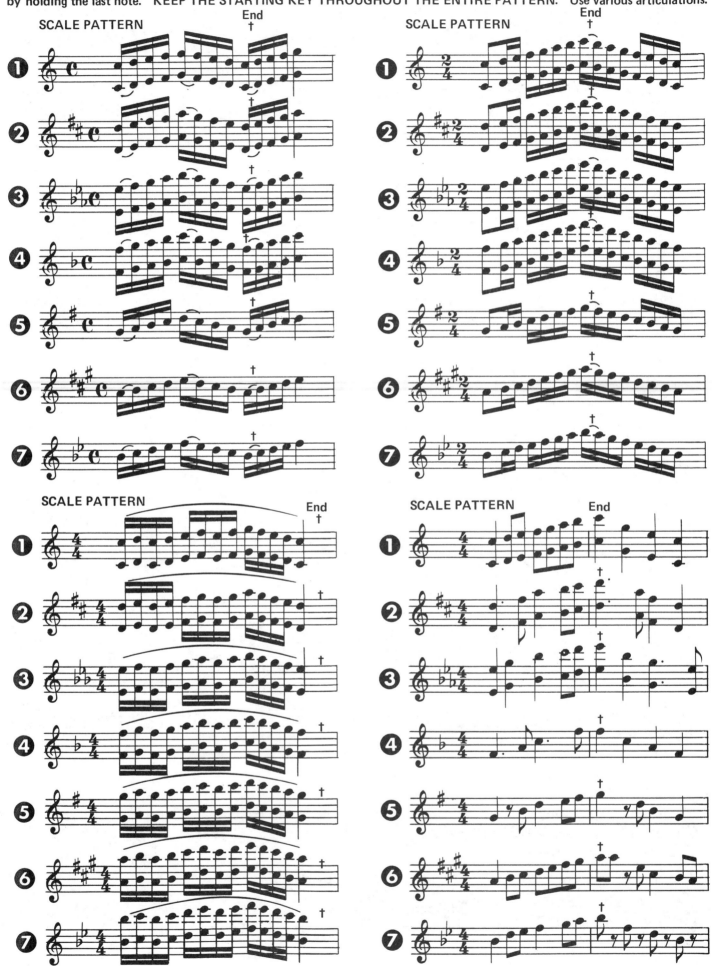

# Themes From Flight Of The Bumble Bee

**This number is presented as a challenge for chromatic development. Work out carefully, then try for speed with accuracy.**

RIMSKY – KORSAKOV

## Summary Of Alternate Fingerings

Below you will find a summary of the most common saxophone alternate fingerings and examples showing in what situation they should be used.

It is very important that you learn to use alternate fingerings in the proper places because as we progress to more difficult music they make it possible to play faster and in a smoother manner. Their use is absolutely essential in more advanced music.